Is There Life Beyon

by David Orme

Contents

Section 1
Are We Alone?	2
Unidentified Flying Objects	6

Section 2
Is There Life on Mars?	12
Europa: Another Place to Look for Life	16

Section 3
Looking for Life in Space	22
Has the Earth Been Visited by Aliens?	27

Glossary	31
Index	32

Edinburgh Gate
Harlow, Essex

Are We Alone?

Many people have looked at the stars and planets and asked if there is life somewhere else in the universe. Many stories have been written about aliens from other worlds visiting the Earth. Sometimes these aliens are not at all friendly!

How can we find out if there is life in space? Can studying life on Earth give us any clues?

Life on Earth

There is life on Earth because the conditions on our planet are just right. The temperature on Earth means that water is liquid – and we do not know of anything that can live without liquid water.

The **atmosphere** on Earth is necessary for life. It protects us from dangerous **radiation** from the sun. The **oxygen** in the atmosphere combines with food to give energy, and helps living things to grow.

The other planets

We cannot find any sign of life on other planets in our **solar system**. Planets such as Jupiter and Saturn are huge "gas giants" – they have deep, poisonous atmospheres.

Planets furthest from the sun are frozen worlds – too cold for life. Mars is a cold dry world, with a very thin atmosphere. Venus and Mercury are far too hot for life. They have temperatures on the surface that would melt lead. When we look at these planets, therefore, it seems that we are the only living things around.

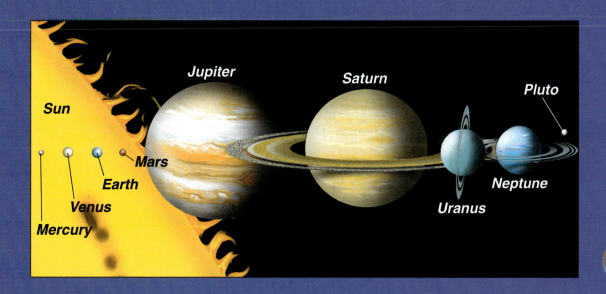

Life can be surprising!

The other planets in the solar system do not look like good places to find life. However, life can survive in many strange places – even on Earth.

Scientists have found living things at the bottom of the sea where there is no sunlight and no oxygen. These creatures get their energy from the heat of underwater volcanoes. They feed on the chemicals in the rocks that the volcano produces.

Deep sea crabs living on a black smoker vent at the bottom of the Atlantic Ocean

Life has been found deep underground, and in the coldest places such as Antarctica. If life can survive in these places then maybe there is life on the other planets after all. Of course, it won't be intelligent life, and it probably won't be paying us a visit!

Imagine that you are sitting on a sandy beach. You pick up a handful of sand and look at the tiny grains. How long would it take to count the grains in just one handful?

Look at the beach stretching away in the distance. Imagine how many lifetimes it would take to count all those grains of sand. Then think about the grains of sand on every beach in the world. It is impossible to imagine a number that is as big as this.

And yet this number isn't nearly as big as the number of stars there are in the universe. Each star is a sun, and may have planets **orbiting** round it. So even if there is no life in the solar system, there could be life beyond it. The problem is, these stars and planets are so far away that even the fastest rocket would take thousands of years to reach them.

Is life in space likely or not?

Somewhere out in space, it is likely that there is other life. There may even be intelligent creatures looking through *their* telescopes at us! The problem is that finding out for certain is difficult. Difficult, but not impossible.

Unidentified Flying Objects

Visits from space

If there is life out in space, then it is possible that there are intelligent creatures somewhere. They could be much further ahead in science than us. They may have invented space ships. They may have even secretly visited us on Earth!

A scene from Close Encounters of the Third Kind

Flying saucers

Many people have seen strange objects in the sky. Some people believe this is proof that aliens from space are visiting us. There are photographs and videos that are said to show "flying saucers". Some of them look very real.

Is this a real flying saucer – or is it fake?

Often the people who see **UFOs** are pilots. They are experts in observation. Sometimes UFOs have been seen by whole groups of people. People in different places have spotted the same UFO as it travels overhead.

Mysterious objects have also been seen on radar screens. We know that they could not be normal aircraft because they travel too fast, and turn far too quickly.

Meeting aliens

There are some people who say they have met and spoken to aliens. They say that they have been inside alien spaceships. Others say that aliens captured them and did experiments on their bodies. There are also stories of aliens taking animals away from farms.

There are a number of descriptions of aliens. The best known are called "greys". They have small bodies, strange triangle-shaped heads and very large eyes.

People who study reports of UFOs are called ufologists. Some ufologists claim that the governments of the world know all about flying saucers. They claim that governments keep what they know secret so that people are not frightened.

Where is the evidence?

It is very difficult to prove that these things are really true. People can make up stories for the fun of it, or for money, or because they want to be well known.

There are many objects in the sky, such as balloons or aeroplanes. When they are seen from strange angles, or in strange light conditions, they can look very odd. Photographs or videos might really be pictures of something quite ordinary. They may even be faked. Even the radar sightings might be caused by equipment that is not working properly.

A fake flying saucer

There is also the problem of distance. Space travel between the stars would take thousands of years … unless there is a way of travel that we haven't discovered yet.

One possible cause of the strange sightings is secret military aircraft. For many years the United States' most secret aircraft was the stealth bomber. While it was being developed, many people saw strange triangle-shaped UFOs. Some of them thought they came from space.

The biggest problem in believing that alien spacecraft have visited the Earth is that there is no real evidence that scientists can study. For example, some ufologists claim that an alien space ship crashed in America in 1946. It was at a place called Roswell, but the remains of the ship mysteriously went missing …

Are they real?

There is no real evidence to prove that alien spacecraft exist. However, so many people have seen objects in the sky that it is difficult to believe they are all making it up, or that they are all mistaken.

The only way we can be certain is if an alien spaceship lands one day in the middle of a city and aliens step out to meet us.

If this happens, let's hope they're friendly!

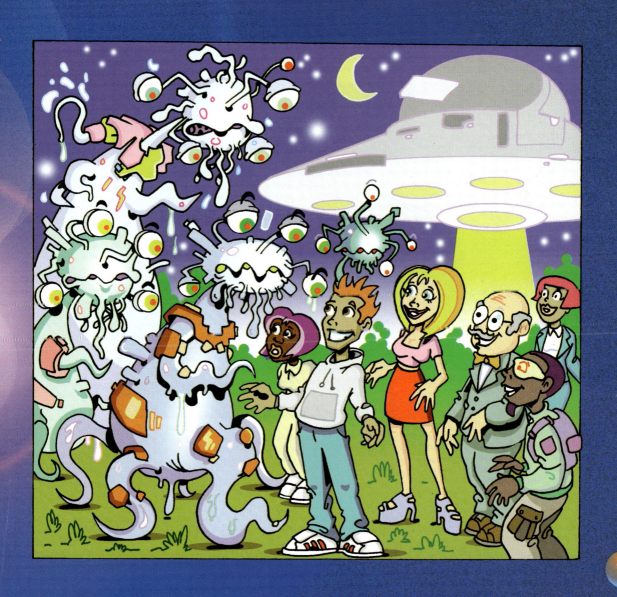

Is There Life on Mars?

For many years **astronomers** thought that Mars was the most likely place in the solar system to find life. Early astronomers even thought that they could see canals on Mars. They thought the canals were a transport system for Martians. Many stories were written about Martians; the best known of these is *The War of the Worlds* by H G Wells.

A scene from War of the Worlds

In recent years **space probes** have allowed us a closer look at the surface of Mars. It was soon discovered that there were no canals – and no sign of life at all! Despite these disappointments, is it still possible that there is life on Mars?

What is it like on Mars?

Mars does not seem a very promising world on which to find life. Human beings could only survive there if they wore space suits, as they do on the moon.

Mars has a very thin atmosphere – only one per cent of the atmosphere on Earth, with very little oxygen. Not only is there no air to breathe, the thin atmosphere would not provide protection from dangerous radiation from the sun.

Mars is a cold and dry planet, with a surface of sand and rocks. Because of the low **air pressure**, any water on the Martian surface would quickly boil away. The average temperature on the surface is -23 degrees Celsius; there is no thick atmosphere to trap the heat of the sun, as happens on Earth.

When you consider all of these facts, Mars does not seem a very likely place to find anything living.

There's just a chance …

Yet despite these facts, scientists haven't given up looking for life on Mars. Recent photographs show dried up water channels on the surface, which proves that there was once water on the surface of Mars. Scientists think that, millions of years ago, Mars may have been warmer and wetter, with a thicker atmosphere.

Channels on a crater wall on Mars

But even if there had been life on Mars, wouldn't it all have died out by now? Some scientists say it may still survive, perhaps underground where the pressure of the rocks prevents water **evaporating**. They say that, on Earth, tiny life forms trapped in ice can survive for thousands of years in a form of **hibernation**. This may be true on Mars as well, but the life forms would be no bigger than tiny bacteria – there are definitely no Martians!

Finding out

The best way to find out if there is life on Mars is to go there and look. It will be many years before astronauts can travel to Mars, but already robots have landed on the planet, and more are on their way. These robots have special tools to look deep in the soil, looking for any traces of life.

There is one other way to look for evidence. In the past, **asteroids** collided with Mars, and chunks of Mars rock were shot out into space. Some of them reached the Earth as **meteorites**. In Antarctica a few years ago, a piece of Martian rock was found. When scientists examined it, they found traces of something that might have been living. Other scientists didn't agree with these findings so we still don't know for sure.

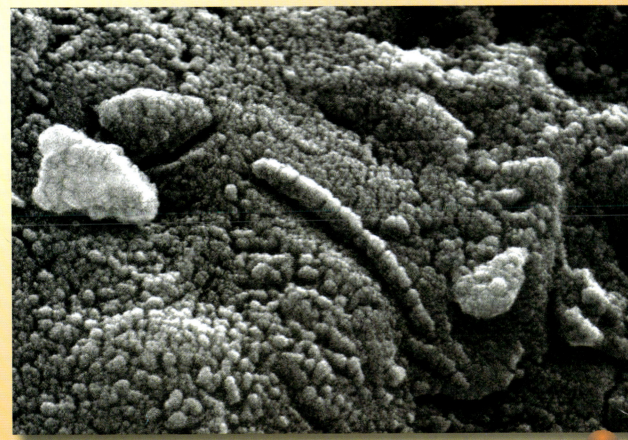

A Martian meteorite

Europa: Another Place to Look for Life

On 9th July 1979 the space probe Voyager 2 passed by **Europa**, which is one of the moons of Jupiter. When photographs of Europa reached Earth, the waiting astronomers were amazed.

The icy surface of Jupiter's moon, Europa

They had expected to see a surface looking like Earth's moon, with rocky mountains and craters. But it was nothing like that. Instead, the surface was bright and smooth. When they looked more closely at the surface they could see that it was covered with cracks.

What was happening on Europa? Could it possibly be a home for life?

The moons of Jupiter

Jupiter is the biggest planet in the solar system, and has at least 17 moons and a feint system of rings. The biggest moon, Ganymede, is very large – in fact, it is larger than Mercury or Pluto.

Jupiter's four largest moons

The moons of Jupiter would not be comfortable places to live. The Jupiter system is almost ten times as far away from the sun as the Earth, so very little heat from the sun reaches it. The moons are not big enough to have a thick atmosphere, and radiation from Jupiter would make the surface dangerous. Jupiter's **gravity** causes "tides" in the rock of the moons, which create huge volcanoes that pour poisonous gases out into space. How could life possibly exist here?

The space probe Galileo

The mystery of Europa

In 1999 the space probe Galileo took more pictures of Europa. Astronomers decided that the strange surface of Europa was probably a thick layer of ice. If that was the case, why was it cracked?

The surface of icy seas on Earth looks quite similar to the surface of Europa. The movement of the sea underneath causes the ice to crack. Could this be the case with Europa? Could Europa have seas underneath the ice?

At first, it seemed impossible. Being so far away from the sun surely all water would be frozen. But what about the volcanoes? If there were underwater volcanoes on Europa, they could make the heat to melt the ice.

Then scientists remembered the strange life that had been found deep in the oceans of Earth. Life had developed near underwater volcanoes, in hot water full of chemicals – in total darkness and with very little oxygen. Could the same thing have happened on Europa?

Finding out

Plans are already being made for an unmanned mission to Europa. A Europa lander would land on the ice, then drill down into the sea below. A small submarine would then explore, looking for any signs of life.

Of course, this mission would be very difficult. However, there is one place on Earth where scientists can practise.

Lake Vostok

In the 1970s a lake about the same size as Lake Ontario in Canada was discovered under the ice of Antarctica. The ice is four kilometres thick, and the water of the lake has been sealed off from the rest of the world for millions of years. The conditions might be very similar to those on Europa. Already scientists are drilling down through the ice to study the water of Lake Vostok. If life is found there, scientists believe there is an excellent chance that life exists on Europa as well!

The drilling tower and laboratory on Lake Vostok

Looking for Life in Space

Scientists are already working on space probes to Mars and **Europa** to see if they can find life there. But how can they find out if there is life anywhere else in the universe?

A space probe in preparation

The problems

Although all stars are suns and could have planets orbiting round them, it used to be thought impossible to find out about life on other worlds because they were just too far away. Firstly, a space probe would take many thousands of years to reach even the nearest star. Secondly, stars are so bright that telescopes cannot pick out planets because they are much less bright and close to their sun. Finding out if there were planets orbiting around other stars was therefore considered to be impossible.

The solutions

However, scientists were determined not to give up that easily. The first idea was to look for life with **radio telescopes** instead of **optical telescopes**. These operate just like a giant radio, except that they are not listening in to radio stations on Earth but for radio signals from space. A giant radio telescope at Mount Arecibo in Puerto Rico is currently collecting radio signals from space. The data received is then analysed to see if any pattern showing intelligent life can be found.

The radio telescope at Mount Arecibo, Puerto Rico

Of course, we can't speak any alien languages, so scientists look for messages that might be written in a common language, such as the language of mathematics. 2 + 2 = 4 is the same everywhere in the universe.

What about non-intelligent life?

It is only intelligent life that could send out radio signals. To discover if any form of life is possible in other places in the universe, scientists first had to establish whether or not there were any planets in orbit around other stars.

Planets travel round the sun in an orbit; they do not fly off into space because of the sun's gravity. Gravity is a force that pulls all things together.

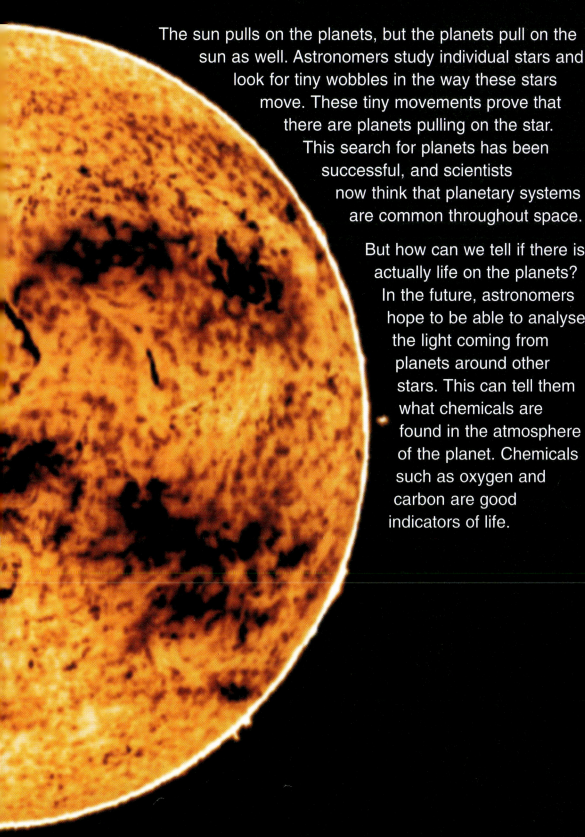

The sun pulls on the planets, but the planets pull on the sun as well. Astronomers study individual stars and look for tiny wobbles in the way these stars move. These tiny movements prove that there are planets pulling on the star. This search for planets has been successful, and scientists now think that planetary systems are common throughout space.

But how can we tell if there is actually life on the planets? In the future, astronomers hope to be able to analyse the light coming from planets around other stars. This can tell them what chemicals are found in the atmosphere of the planet. Chemicals such as oxygen and carbon are good indicators of life.

Why are we looking for life in space?

Some people think that the search for life is a waste of time and money, and would prefer the money spent to be used to help solve some of the problems on Earth. Other scientists argue that finding other living beings in space would be the most important discovery in the history of science.

What do you think?

Listening to the stars

Has the Earth Been Visited by Aliens?

It has not yet been proved that Unidentified Flying Objects come from space, and most scientists do not believe in visiting aliens. However, there are people who believe that evidence for space visitors can be found in the history of the Earth.

Ancient spacemen?

Some people believe that many of the things created by ancient people, such as the pyramids in Egypt or ancient cities in South America, could not have been built by human beings. They say that only an advanced technology could lift huge blocks of stone and put them in the correct place. They look at old writings that mention things such as gods in flying chariots and claim that the ancient writers are really talking about aliens in spaceships!

The pyramids at Giza, Egypt

The science of **archaeology** has disproved most of these theories by finding out how ancient people really did manage to create wonderful monuments. Just because someone lived hundreds or even thousands of years ago, doesn't mean they weren't as clever as us. Inventing a theory, then looking around for facts to fit it, is not good science. Good scientists start with facts based on observations, then they try and work out theories to explain them and link them together.

Real aliens

Not many scientists believe stories about aliens in spaceships. But some have found evidence to prove that alien life has visited Earth – and is still visiting it, unnoticed, to this day!

The theory

On 20th April 1967, the **unmanned lunar lander** Surveyor 3 landed on the surface of the moon. One of the things aboard was a television camera. Two-and-a-half years later, on 20th November 1969, **Apollo 12** astronauts Pete Conrad and Alan L. Bean recovered the camera. When **NASA** scientists examined it back on Earth they were amazed to find specimens of bacteria on the camera that were still alive, and which must have been there before the Surveyor 3 was launched. It seemed impossible, but these bacteria had survived for 31 months on the moon!

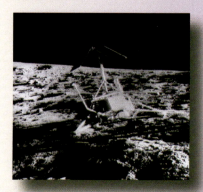

Surveyor 3

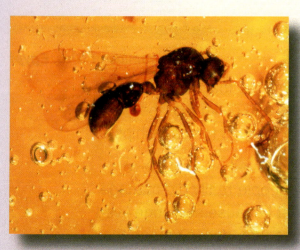

An insect trapped in amber

On Earth there are many examples of bacteria surviving for long periods. Living bacteria thirty million years old have been found sealed inside **prehistoric amber**. Other samples have been found in ancient ice. Bacteria are almost impossible to destroy.

Comet tails

Astronomers have discovered many of the important chemicals that are building blocks for life in the tails of **comets**. The tail of a comet is material from the comet itself, which is being boiled off by the heat of the sun. The Earth often passes through the tail of comets, and dust is trapped in the atmosphere.

Some scientists now believe that chemicals that can create life, and even bacteria, might arrive on Earth from comets, or even in the centre of meteorites. They think that this is how life on Earth started. Ancient people believed that meteor showers were signs that disease was on its way. Some scientists believe that they were absolutely right, and that new diseases might originate in space.

Other investigators are not convinced, arguing that life originated in the sea, and that bacteria from space could not possibly reach Earth. But if the theory is true, and this is how life began, then there are aliens on Earth – us!

Glossary

air pressure — the force pushing on us by the air around us

Apollo 12 — the second manned mission to the moon

archaeology — the study of objects from the past

asteroids — "mini planets" ranging in size from a few metres to 300 kilometres in diameter

atmosphere — the air around a planet

astronomers — people who study the stars and planets

comets — large masses of ice and dust that travel in regular orbits around the sun

Europa — one of the planet Jupiter's moons

evaporating — turning from liquid into gas

gravity — the force that pulls things towards each other

hibernation — the ability of some living things to spend long periods of time in deep sleep, with few or no signs of life

meteorites — rocks which reach the surface of the Earth from space

NASA — National Aeronautics and Space Administration – the organisation that organises America's space missions

optical telescopes — telescopes with lenses that make distant objects seem larger and nearer

oxygen — a gas found in the air which is essential to life

orbiting — travelling round an object such as a sun in a regular path

prehistoric amber — Amber is a form of gum that oozes from trees. It can become hard and survive for millions of years. Sometimes tiny insects and other forms of life can be trapped inside.

radiation — rays given out by the sun and by radioactive objects; some rays, such as cosmic rays, can be dangerous to life and astronauts need spacesuits to protect themselves

radio telescopes — giant receivers that collect various sorts of rays, such as radio and X-rays, from space

solar system — the sun and the planets, and moons that orbit around them

space probes — unmanned space ships containing equipment to study space, planets, etc.

UFOs — Unidentified Flying Objects – anything seen in the sky that cannot be identified for certain

unmanned lunar lander — a lunar lander is the part of a space ship that lands on the moon; an unmanned lander has no people in it

Index

aliens	2, 8, 27–30
amber	28
America	10
Antarctica	4, 15, 20
Apollo 12	28
asteroids	15
Atlantic Ocean	4
atmosphere	3
comet	29
Egypt	27
Europa	16–21, 22
flying saucers	7, 8
Galileo	19
Ganymede	17
greys	8
Jupiter	3, 16, 17
Lake Vostok	20
Mars	3, 12–15, 22
Martians	14
Mercury	3, 17
meteorites	15
Mount Arecibo	23
NASA	28
oxygen	3, 4
Pluto	17
radiation	3
radio signals	23, 24
Roswell	10
Saturn	3
solar system	3, 5, 17
South America	27
stealth bomber	10
sun	5, 13, 24–25
Surveyor 3	28
UFOs	6–11
Venus	3
volcano	4, 19
Voyager 2	16
Wells, H G	12